THE LATEST
HERMAN

by Jim Unger

ANDREWS, McMEEL & PARKER
A Universal Press Syndicate Company
KANSAS CITY • NEW YORK

ISBN: 0-8362-1168-5

Library of Congress Catalog Card
Number: 81-065137

First printing, April 1981
Eighth printing, February 1985

"Strange how all six of your
previous employers left the 'C' out
of the word 'excellent'."

"Keep it to yourself, but
I've finished spending that $5
you gave me for Christmas."

"Please don't slurp that soup whilst I'm trying to watch the movie."

"Dear Diary, the old skinflint forgot my allowance again."

"That was either Superman or
dad falling off the roof."

"It must have been that time your
brother brought his portable over!"

"If you ever eat turkey, you're a cannibal!"

"This one turns men into putty!"

"If you want the inside cleaned, just
leave your windows down."

"Did you tell the dog he couldn't
go out tonight?"

"I've got to ask the boss for a raise
tomorrow. How does this look?"

"If he's your brother, sir, I'm sure I
would have remembered him."

"I can't figure it. These carrot plants
are getting smaller!"

"He's half parrot and half homing
pigeon. I've sold him ten times!"

"Not Walter . . . WATER!"

"This is one I did on
my trip to Australia."

"I'm gonna use this ball. I keep losing
the other ones."

APARTMENT
FOR RENT

"D'you think we really
need a kitchen?"

"Can we have our horseshoe back?"

"Now, which pile was washed
in 'Sudsy-Wudsy'?"

"This is not the bank!"

"You seem to have the qualifications
we're looking for in a bookkeeper."

"Have you got a medium-sized hummingbird?"

"I told you that was HIS chair!"

"My husband kept telling me to drive faster, Officer."

"One of these hot dogs fell on the floor. You'll have to toss a coin!"

"Back to the drawing board, smarty-pants!"

"We've got 60 guests and only three pieces of cake!"

"I'd let you talk more, but you're not as interesting as me."

"Where's that dumb cat?"

"Which one of you
is General Smith?"

"They shouldn't be showing
girls in bikinis when kids
his age are watching!"

"How come you don't go fishing
anymore?"

"It's not egg on toast.
It's egg OR toast!"

"Be fair! He did ask you twice to take it off."

"You can't expect me to learn the job in five minutes, can you?"

"We haven't seen a duck for two hours!"

"I need as much fire insurance as I can get by next Friday night."

"Got any books with nice, big, colored pictures in them, suitable for framing?"

"That guy who's filling in for you at the office is a real worker."

"I never did like dogs!"

"There are more than eight
cornflakes in there!"

"Did you say that guy next door joined the Army?"

"That's nice! You show up and all the gorillas run inside."

"I gave your sandwich to the wrong
customer. Do you still want it?"

"I put two eggs in this cake!"

"You'd better let the cat in before he
wakes up the street."

"That's what it says: 'one
tablespoonful, 300 times a day.'"

"The doctor won't be long. Are you sure you wouldn't like a cup of coffee?"

"Joe's my bodyguard till I tell you where I've been all night."

"What are you asking me for?"

"This is 'Earth.' We don't hang around here too long — they're all bananas."

"Tell Sandra, lover-boy is here."

"When I said you could have your
friends over for lunch, I meant
humans."

"I want you to know I'm a firm
supporter of the ERA."

"I don't think all that natural food is
doing you any good!"

"The car wash never gets it clean."

"If I bought your burglar alarm for
$30, it would be the only thing in
here worth stealing."

"I was lucky I hit the pin!"

"I don't know what this is, but it's new and improved, so it must be good!"

"When I told him it would be nice to have my breakfast in bed once in a while, he told me to sleep in the kitchen."

"Let's hope we never have to use it!"

"Ho, ho, ho."

"I have to be in bed at eight, so get there about five minutes past."

"It was a great party, Ralph."

"I think we'll get out of here before
the cowboy movie starts."

"He's been filling it with food for 47 years!"

"Do you want to drive now?"

"Your wife's still standing in the doorway."

"Where did you get these eggs?"

"Operator, how do I make a long-distance call from here?"

"Why don't you listen? I said bring me a WENCH."

"Stop him! He's got your dinner."

"You must be hearing things; my phone wasn't ringing."

"There's a F-I-L-E in the C-A-K-E."

"Looking at you, I'd guess your wife doesn't have exceptionally good taste!"

"Six boxes of cookies for you, and no arguments."

"Excuse me. The machine is making a funny noise and the little light is going in a straight line."

"Keep an eye on that one."

"She was doing her TV exercises and has been stuck there through three soap operas!"

"What's the big idea telling my wife you're getting a new dishwasher?"

"Can't you keep still?"

"Don't try to tell me my job! That's
No. 37!"

"Do you take trade-ins?"

"I'm still not getting any hot water!"

"This stew is ruined. You said you'd
be home last year!"

"'Buttercup' recognized your car coming and ran off."

"I keep the door locked. I can't understand how they all got in there!"

"I can't stand the sight of blood."

"I made you a nice fruitcake, but the guard said it could be used as an offensive weapon."

"You heard me! Take your hat off."

"Smoking or non-smoking?"

"See what happens when you find them not guilty?"

"What do you want for your birthday, a battery-tester or a set of screwdrivers?"

"Take two of these with meals but no more than 30 a day."

"I was practicing my karate and she hit me with half a brick."

"Your teeth have gone in my jello!"

"I think you're probably in a rut."

"Good luck!"

"I hope you haven't got gravy all over your shoes."

"How far can I send this cat for 30 dollars?"

"What's my whisk doing in here?"

"Going anywhere near the tropics?"

"I've studied your case and I think
your best bet is a tunnel!"

"You'll have to sit up!"

"You'll have to wait for your soup. I can't do everything!"

"This won't take long, will it? The first race starts in 20 minutes."

"What are you doing?"

"Those two seem to be enjoying themselves."

"I thought you were gonna clean up this kitchen."

"Members of the jury, I must ask you to disregard my last remark."

"Here's your watch, Johnson. You're retiring early."

"Testing . . . testing."

"I don't want to be a 'lookout' ANYMORE."

"I don't know whether to try to
weed the lawn or tell everyone
it's a vegetable garden."

"Dad, do I get my allowance or not?"

"D'you want a dessert or coffee?"

"Don't be a spoilsport! Guess who it is."

"Have a good vacation, Wilson?"

"This may be out of your price range. It's $2."

"I want you to take a half-hour walk,
every day, 10 minutes before lunch."

"I came in third!"

"I told you it was a dog movie!"

"He never said that!
I saw your lips move."

"Wanna buy a toothbrush?"

**"Is that the dress you wore
on our honeymoon?"**

"Are they the new shoes you bought for $10?"

"They ALWAYS go on the warpath when we're eating!"

"Have you given any thought to my pay raise?"

"You told me on the phone that you were a six-footer!"

"I had the spaghetti yesterday and
my stomach's still working on it!"

"SIT!"

"Do you want the book
of instructions?"

"You won't be losing a daughter.
We're going to live here!"

"Have you seen the latest
electric model?"

"I'd say it's your gall bladder, but
if you insist on a second opinion,
I'll say kidneys."

"My mistake. I'm supposed to
rub it on your chest."

"He'll never find the cigars,
will he, Dad?"

"Can you send a tow truck?
I'm about 300 yards inside the
Lion Safari Park."

**"Dad's gonna change the baby.
I hope he gets a dog!"**

"Have you been waiting long?"

"I wouldn't pay $4 admission
to look at you!"

"These TV commercials are
getting ridiculous!"

"My ball went in the hole!
What shall I do now?"

"I think we'll stay away from
the jumbo-burger!"

"Twenty bucks a week on makeup, and he's the best you can come up with?"

"I see on your application that you used to be a termite inspector."

"Is hernia catching, Herm?"

"Stay there. I got the wrong one."

"Your head's rejecting your hair transplant!"

"How many times have I told you not to start moving till I get my glasses on?"

"One step closer and I'll soak you to the skin."

"Why don't you have a good scream and get it over with."

"He hates it when someone uses his bowl."

"I can't understand a word he says! Try him in Spanish."

"You were sleepwalking again last night."

"Of course it's empty! I had to hide everything."

"I never said a word. He said it!"

"I finally got a day off!"

"You said it was getting tired. It's gone to bed!"

"Don't keep whistling."

"Don't look at me like that. It's 'evolution.'"

"I changed the baby. Now what?"

"Your wife's been away for three weeks now. Have you had anything to eat?"

"Have the hamburger on the house. You're the first customer who ever came back!"

"I think I prefer the blue."

"I want a book on speed-reading and 85 Westerns."

"Make sure this one doesn't leave
before he pays his bill."

"I see you giving me a $20 tip!"

"Have you been at my sherry
again, Wilkins?"

LUGGAGE

"That one's genuine crocodile!"

"We don't usually accept first-grade students until they're five years old."

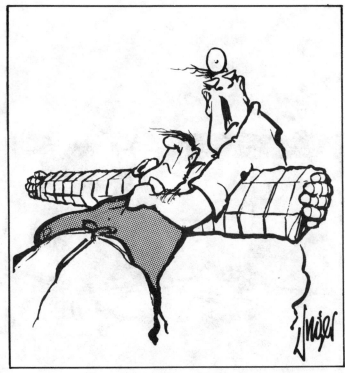

"Close that door!"

"You can't miss, Georgy."

"I'll cook you a nice three-course
meal during the next commercial."

"I think you've overwatered it!"

"Let me know if you ever need a good defense lawyer."

"Even I can paint better than that!"

"Harry, the Earth isn't the third planet from the sun, is it?"

"My bus leaves in two minutes and
I intend to be on it."

"He's got my tuna fish
sandwiches again!"

"He's chewed through the TV cord again!"

"As it was a false alarm, I'll just give you one quick squirt."